Tune Book

POCKETBOOK DELUXE SERIES
by William Bay

1 2 3 4 5 6 7 8 9 0

Visit us on the Web at www.melbay.com — E-mail us at email@melbay.com

2   Table of Contents

4 Green Grow the Lilacs

Soprano Recorder Fingering Chart

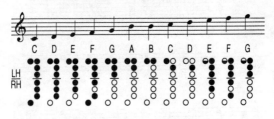

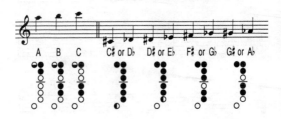

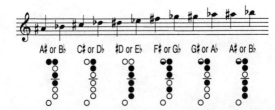

Tenting Tonight

Aloha Oe

Lament

The Foggy, Foggy Dew

The Ash Grove

One More River

Auld Lang Syne

Strawberry Roan

Johnny Has Gone
for a Soldier

Ol' Dan Tucker

Blow Away
the Morning Dew

Bell Bottom Trousers

Old Shoe Boots
& Leggins

Wait Till the Sun Shines
Nellie

At a Georgia Camp Meeting

Marchin' to Glory

Goin' South

Oh, Sinner Man

Come & Go with Me
to that Land

Bile' Dem Cabbage Down ²⁵

Goober Peas

Captain Kidd

The Fish of the Sea

Jolly Old Roger

My Bonnie

The Bold Fisherman

High Barbaree

Greenland Fishery

Blow, Ye Winds

Cripple Creek

Sourwood Mountain

Big Rock Candy Mountain

The Roving Cowboy

When Jesus Wept

Blessed Quietness

There's a River of Life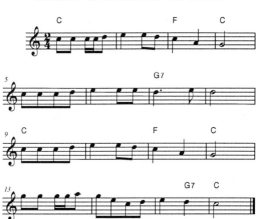

When I Can Read
My Title Clear

Early American

Praise the Savior

German

Great God When I
Approach Thy Throne

Early American

Must Jesus Bear The Cross Alone

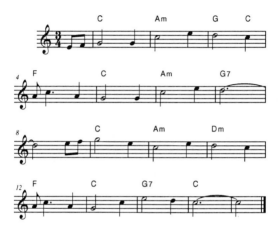

I am Bound for the Promised Land

When Jesus Left His Father's Throne

Jesus Calls Us

Lonesome Valley

The Galway Races

Cockles & Mussels

The Wild Rover

Love is Teasin'

The Galway Shawl

The Rose of Tralee

Brain O'linn

Spancil Hill

Si Beag Si Mór

Bunclody

My Mary of the Curling Hair

Musetta's Waltz

Drink to Me Only
with Thine Eyes

Southern Roses

Strauss

Gypsy Theme

Hatikvoh

Israeli

66

Santa Lucia

Neopolitan Song

Tis So Sweet

Gospel Song

68 I Need Thee Every Hour

Gospel Song

Precious Memories

Gospel Song

70

Mandy Lee

Slowly

American Ballad

Daisy Bell

Up in a Balloon

Lively

Strike Up the Band

Lively March

74 This Little Light of Mine

Silver Threads
Among the Gold

Grandfather's Clock

All God's Children Got Shoes

Little David Play on Your Harp

Spiritual

If You're Happy
and You Know it

I've Got Peace
Like a River

Spiritual

Bringing in the Sheaves 81

Gospel Song

In the Pines

The Battle Cry of Freedom

Nine Hundred Miles

Down Where the Cotton
Blossoms Grow

Lively Tempo

American Song

America the Beautiful

Our Boys Will Shine Tonight

Columbia, the Gem of the Ocean

Mama Don't 'Low

She'll be Comin' Round the Mountain

Loch Lomond

Crawdad Song

The Mermaid

Lively

American Sailing Song

The Old Oaken Bucket

95

Doxology